LET'S TALK ABOUT

Early Childhood
Social-Emotional Development

Books by the Authors

Embracing Autism in Preschool
Updated Second Edition
Karen Griffin Roberts, M.Ed.

Let's Talk Series

Let's Talk About Autism in Early Childhood
Karen Griffin Roberts, M.Ed.

Let's Talk About Early Language Development
Ana Gamarra Hoover, M.Ed. and Karen Griffin Roberts, M.Ed.

*Let's Talk About Early Childhood Social-Emotional
Development*
Karen Griffin Roberts, M.Ed. and Ana Gamarra Hoover, M.Ed.

LET'S TALK ABOUT
Early Childhood
Social-Emotional Development

Karen Griffin Roberts, M.Ed.
Ana Gamarra Hoover, M.Ed.

Fourth Lloyd Productions, LLC
Burgess, VA

For permissions write to:
Fourth Lloyd Productions, LLC
512 Old Glebe Point Road
Burgess, VA 22432
email: 4thLloyd@gmail.com
www.FourthLloydProductions.com

ISBN: 978-0-9889391-9-6 paperback

Library of Congress Control Number: 2020938456

Printed in the United States of America

CONTENTS

Foreword 7
Acknowledgements 11
Children Learn What They Live 13
Introduction 15

Chapter ONE

Ages and Stages of Social-Emotional Development 17
  Social-Emotional Milestones 19
  Temperament 22
  Temperament Versus Emotion 23

Chapter TWO

Social-Emotional Competence 25
Dimensions of Social-Emotional Competence 27
Self-Esteem and Self-Confidence 28
  Separation Anxiety 29
  Always Say Goodbye 29
  Validate Your Child's Feelings 30
  Praise Versus Encouragement 30
  Everyone Makes Mistakes 32
  Feelings and Emotions 32
  Self-Control and Self-Regulation 33
  Mistakes Versus Misbehavior 34
  Follow Routines 35
  Down Time 36
  Disrupted Routines 36
  Give Children Choices 37
  Speak in the Positive 37
  Be Consistent 38

Chapter THREE
Social Skills and Interaction *39*

Development of Social Skills *41*
    Theory of Mind *41*
    Social Skills *41*
    How Children Learn Social Skills *42*
    Developing Friendships *43*
    Sharing *44*
    Put Special Toys in a Special Place *45*
    Following Rules *45*
    Ask for More Time in Responding to Some Requests *46*

Chapter FOUR
Red Flags in Social-Emotional Development *49*
    Red Flags in Social-Emotional Development *51*
        Separation Anxiety *51*
        Social Concerns *51*
    Behavioral Problems *51*
    Difficulty with Transitions Between Activities *52*
    Excessive Clingingness or Attention-Seeking with Adults *52*
    Attention Concerns *52*
    Daily Functioning Concerns *52*
    School Concerns *53*
    Challenging Behavior *53*
    Preparation and Collaboration with Medical and School Professionals *54*
    Attention-Seeking Behavior *55*
    Screen Time *57*

Our Advice to Parents About Early Social-Emotional Development *62*

Appendix A: Suggestions for Further Reading *64*
Appendix B: Fun Ways to Say Goodbye *66*
References *69*
About the Authors *71*

Foreword

As a long-time student, teacher and researcher of human social behavior and cognition, I recognize the value of providing children with the tools they need for healthy relationships with others. Essentially, we are all lifelong students of social-emotional behavior. We've all had the misfortune of misreading or not understanding the reactions or behavior of others in response to our own behavior. *Why did he do that? Why did she say that to me? Why is he so upset? What are they thinking that caused them to react that way?* And the younger one is, the more likely that is, as children are only beginning to develop the capacity to navigate their social worlds. We also experience times when we don't understand our own behavior or feelings. *Why did I say that? What was I thinking when I did that? Why didn't I do 'this' instead of 'that?'* Without insight into why they feel as they do, or the words to express their feelings, children can be very frustrated and confused by the social arena. And for children without strong and consistent models of appropriate social behavior and emotion expression, difficulties can arise. Sometimes it's the parents who are having difficulties with normal but developmentally immature reactions of children; they expect more from their children than they are capable of at that stage of development. *Let's Talk About Early Childhood Social-Emotional Development* provides a concise and clearly written summary of how to provide children with the tools they need for healthy social-emotional development.

This book is intimately tied to previous books in this series, *Let's Talk About Early Language Development* (Hoover & Roberts, 2013) and *Let's Talk About Autism in Early Childhood* (Roberts, 2014). All three books follow the same format with summaries of research findings in relevant areas, followed by common questions or concerns that parents have about the development of their children. As in the previous texts, Roberts and Hoover provide elegant examples and, in direct and clearly-written language, provide strategies for helping children with behaviors that parents or teachers find problematic.

In the present book, Roberts and Hoover describe the processes involved in developing relationships with others and in regulating one's emotions. Chapter 1 provides an overview of social-emotional milestones in development and a discussion of the distinction between temperament and emotion. The authors emphasize the child's need to learn to self-regulate emotional responses and the importance of positive role models to that process. Chapter 2 describes the development of social-emotional competence and its dependence on attachment early in life. The importance of self-confidence, self-control and self-regulation of behavior and emotions are coupled with suggestions for increasing a child's ability to develop appropriate behavior and emotional responses. Chapter 3 presents information on a child's development of social skills and healthy relationships, and ways parents can enhance this development and address issues that might arise for their children. The final chapter considers "red flags," or particular concerns parents may have for the social-emotional development of their child. Roberts and Hoover stress the need for communication with the child, for communication between parents and teachers, and for professional help when deemed necessary. The authors provide a helpful list of resources for parents or teachers who may want more information or to make contact with a professional for more assistance.

This book is of benefit to parents and teachers alike who struggle with, or have questions about what healthy social-emotional development looks like. In all, I find the positive approach taken by Roberts and Hoover to be refreshing. They stress consistently the need to talk to your child, share with your child, and provide a positive role-model for his or her social-emotional development. The strategies suggested throughout the text are practical tools that can be easily implemented by parents and teachers. The authors have emphasized repeatedly the need for collaboration and consistency in approaches between parents and teachers in this process. With the knowledge and sensitivity they have developed through years of experiences, these two experts in early-child development have provided a clearly written, easily understood, and plausible approach to dealing with questions and concerns parents and teachers have about the social-emotional development of children. I highly recommend this book, as well as the previous two books in this series, to parents and teachers alike.

Judith G. Chapman, Ph.D.
Social Psychology
Emeritus Professor of Psychology, Saint Joseph's University

Acknowledgements

This is the final book in our "Let's Talk Series." All of the three books in the series are dedicated to our own families, and to the many families who through the years have shared with us their children's developmental experiences. We are blessed for having had the privilege of working side by side and heart to heart with families during a wonderful time in their young children's development.

We are grateful to everyone who helped to advance this book series project and to those who encouraged its continuance. Our thanks to those who provided us with their invaluable expertise, including Dr. Judith Chapman for her Foreword, and to Kristen Scott, Erin Saar, Tiffany Atienza, Margie Talbot and Robert Chapman for their reviews. We are especially grateful to Stephanie Hanley for reading the rough draft to give us a better understanding of a parent's view, and to Mary Fannin, who has read through each book in the series and fixed typos and grammatical errors that—even after several reads and re-reads—we never would have found!

Finally, we would not have seen this book series to fruition, had it not been for the artwork, design and publishing advice received from Richard and Nancy Stodart of Fourth Lloyd Productions. And, loving thanks to our husbands who continued to fill in the gaps of family schedules as we sat for hours at our computers trying to put into words for young children's families our views and our understanding on all issues surrounding areas of early childhood development.

Children Learn What They Live

If children live with criticism, they learn to condemn.

If children live with hostility, they learn to fight.

If children live with fear, they learn to be apprehensive.

If children live with pity, they learn to feel sorry for themselves.

If children live with ridicule, they learn to feel shy.

If children live with jealousy, they learn to feel envy.

If children live with shame, they learn to feel guilty.

If children live with encouragement, they learn confidence.

If children live with tolerance, they learn patience.

If children live with praise, they learn appreciation.

If children live with acceptance, they learn to love.

If children live with approval, they learn to like themselves.

If children live with recognition, they learn it is good to have a goal.

If children live with sharing, they learn generosity.

If children live with honesty, they learn truthfulness.

If children live with fairness, they learn justice.

If children live with kindness and consideration, they learn respect.

If children live with security, they learn to have faith in themselves
and in those about them.

If children live with friendliness, they learn the world is a nice
place in which to live.

— *Dorothy Law Nolte*

Excerpted from the book CHILDREN LEARN WHAT THEY LIVE © 1988 by Dorothy Law Note and Rachel Harris. The poem "Children Learn What They Live" © 1972 by Dorothy Law Nolte. Used by permission of Workman Publishing Co., Inc, New York. All Rights Reserved.

With gratitude to the family of Dorothy Law Nolte for continuing her legacy through their website: www.childrenlearnwhattheylive.com

Introduction

S ocial-emotional development is an important predictor of success for a person from early childhood through adulthood. We are all social beings, and the connections and associations we make and how we perceive and act on them in our daily lives, impact our emotional well-being and shape our character.

As early childhood special educators, we are intimately familiar with the many questions and concerns that arise when parents feel that their child's social-emotional development is challenged. Topics addressing behaviors and social-emotional competencies are sought out regularly and well attended at parent and teacher professional development seminars. Indeed, when we first decided to write this book, we put it off far too long because each time we contemplated its contents, we were overwhelmed with resources, research, and the strategies we continually update as we reflect upon our own visions of "positive guidance" in our classrooms.

As the third and final book in the "Let's Talk" series, this book may share some similarities with our earlier publications, *Let's Talk About Early Language Development (Fourth Lloyd Productions, 2013)* and *Let's Talk About Autism in Early Childhood* (Fourth Lloyd Productions, 2014). These topics were chosen for the series because, as special educators, we believe that language and communication, daily experiences and challenges, individual perceptions and styles, and social-emotional development are intricately woven to mold a person's individuality and character.

The information we present in this book is drawn from our experiences as special educators. While we are not behavior specialists, we have assisted behavior specialists in drafting and implementing intervention plans for students in our classrooms. And, while this book provides a brief introduction and cannot possibly address all areas of early social-emotional development, it is the hope of the authors that it will provide families with a better understanding of the many processes involved in developing social skills, positive behaviors and emotional self-regulation. As you wish to learn more about specific areas of early social-emotional development, we invite you to review the recommended reading resources at the end of this book.

ONE

Ages and Stages of
Social-Emotional Development

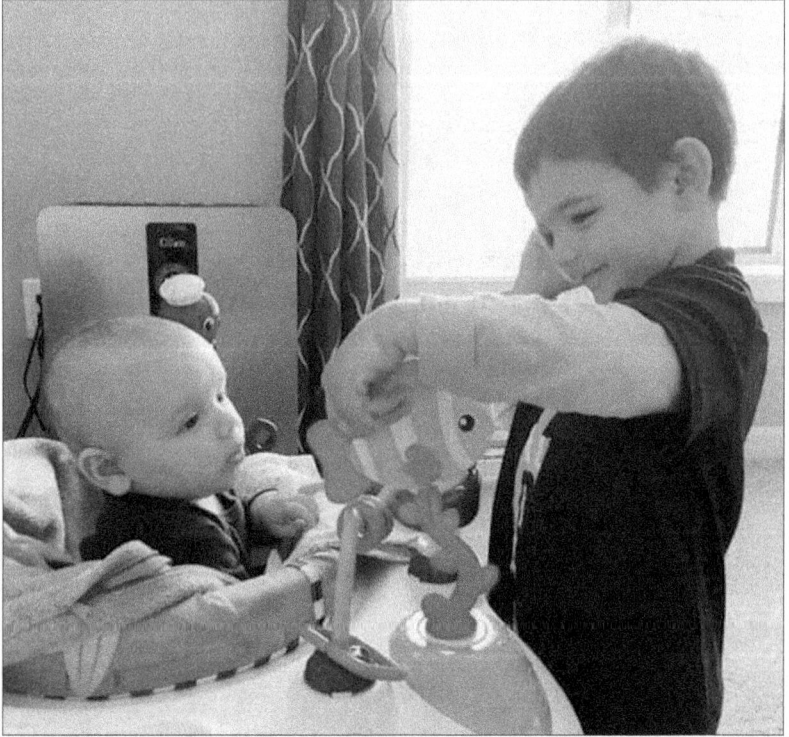

Social-Emotional Milestones

How do I know my child's social-emotional skills are, or are not, developing appropriately?

As with all areas of development, social-emotional development is tracked against an average of other children your child's age. And, as with all developmental milestones, social-emotional skills are developed consistent with the child's own behavior patterns and at the child's own pace.

Let's help you to better understand some concerns or questions parents might have by taking a look at the following social-emotional milestones (Morin, 2020).

Infant

By 2 months

- Cries to get needs met
- Self-soothes by occasionally sucking on hands and fingers
- Begins to smile and looks directly at you

By 4 months

- Cries in different ways to show hunger, pain, or being tired
- Smiles in response to caregiver's smile
- Plays with toys by shaking them

By 6 months

- More aware of familiar people versus strangers
- Responds to the emotions of others by crying, smiling, or laughing
- Enjoys looking at self in the mirror

By 9 months

- Begins to show stranger anxiety

- May cry when familiar faces aren't around

- Starts to prefer some toys over others

By 12 months

- Plays favorites with familiar people

- Is more interactive (like handing over a toy or a book or making a specific noise to get a caregiver's attention)

- Enjoys simple interactive games, like patty-cake and peekaboo

Toddler and Preschool

Age 18-months–2 years

- Has more temper tantrums and becomes more defiant as they try to communicate and be independent

- Starts simple pretend play, like imitating what adults or other kids are doing

- Becomes interested in having other kids around, but is more likely to play alongside them (parallel play) than with them (cooperative play)

Age 3–4 years

- Begins to show and verbalize a wider range of emotion

- Is interested in pretend play, but may confuse real and "make believe"

- Is spontaneously kind and caring

- Begins playing with other kids and separates from caregivers more easily

- May still have tantrums because of changes in routine or not getting needs met

Elementary School Age

Age 5–6 years

- Enjoys playing with other kids and is more conversational and independent

- Tests boundaries but is still eager to please and help out

- Begins to understand what it means to feel embarrassed

Age 7–8 years

- Is more aware of others' perceptions

- May complain about friendships and other kids' reactions

- Wants to behave well, but isn't as attentive to directions

- Tries to express feelings with words, but may resort to aggression when upset

Age 9–10 years

- Shares secrets and jokes with friends

- May start to develop own identity by withdrawing from family activities and conversations

- Is affectionate, silly, and curious, but can also be selfish, rude, and argumentative

Our six-month old seems to always be fussy. Neither my husband nor I have much of a temper, so it is very difficult to understand. How is this possible?

Temperament

Temperament is innate; meaning each child is born with his own temperament. Researchers often refer to temperaments as either "easy" or "difficult" or "slow to warm up" (Trawick-Smith, 2006). Researchers (Allen & Cowdery, 2015) also suggest that there are nine dimensions to temperament. They include:

1. *Activity level:* High, medium, or quiet;

2. *Distractibility:* A child's ability to concentrate in the midst of environmental activity;

3. *Intensity:* Energy level of a child's response—either positive or negative;

4. *Regularity:* Predictability of biological functions;

5. *Sensory Threshold:* The amount of stimulation required to get a response;

6. *Approach/Withdrawal:* A child's typical response to a new situation;

7. *Adaptability:* A child's ease in adjusting to transitions and changes in routine;

8. *Persistence:* The length of time a child continues an activity after encountering difficulty; and

9. *Mood:* A child's tendency to react to the world in a positive or negative way.

These temperaments are seen throughout a child's development, even into adulthood, guiding a person's social-emotional health.

I don't understand. What is the difference between temperament and emotion?

Temperament Versus Emotion

As we indicated earlier, each person is born with an underlying temperament; as unique as his own developing personality. On the other hand, behavior specialists (Harvey & Penzo, 2009) describe emotions as being either primary or secondary. They describe primary emotions as biological and automatic emotional reactions to an incident--such as fear or sadness. We don't need to learn to fear objects or events that could be harmful to us, nor do we need to learn to feel sad when we are upset. While we have little control over primary emotions, we can learn how to adjust and react to secondary emotions.

The specialists (Harvey & Penzo, 2009), describe secondary emotions as reactions based on initial beliefs or assumptions. For instance, you become angry when you get a call from the school nurse to come pick up your ill daughter. This is the fourth time in two weeks you've had to leave work and take her home. And, in each of the other instances, your daughter showed no ill symptoms once you were home. You storm into the nurse's office and learn that your daughter has spiked a fever of 102 degrees. You are no longer angry, but embarrassed for entering the office with such anger, and are worried about your daughter's health. Secondary emotions are described here as the angry emotion giving way to embarrassment and worry; reactions to your first emotion. It is these secondary emotions which we are able to learn to control. Learning is the key element here. Children require guidance in this area to learn how to self-regulate emotional intensity so that they do not get stuck for long periods of time in anger or other potentially destructive emotional states.

Understand that emotions can be positive or negative, give pleasure or discomfort, might last for longer or shorter periods of time and swing as moods change (Changing Minds, 2018). Emotions present as highs and lows in one's feelings and bring on more immediate visible responses to the emotion a person might be feeling such as loving responses, laughing, crying, temper tantrums, etc. Temperament is part of an individual's personality and it is the basic foundation for emotions (Changing Minds, 2018).

Do you mean that since my son was born with a difficult temperament, he will continue to be short-tempered and show more emotion?

Research (NSCC, 2004) confirms emotions are drawn from biological temperament. Therefore, just as temperament varies from person to person, so will the way a person controls his emotions in different situations. For instance, there is research to indicate that people with developmental delays often feel emotions more intensely (Roberts, 2014). So, in answer to your question: Yes, your son will likely feel and show more emotion than the average child. However, take heart in knowing that emotions are also shaped by relationships with others (Trawick-Smith, 2006). Research into social-emotional development (Zero to Three, 2010) strongly suggests that positive relationships not only help children learn to trust others, but healthy relationships help children develop a sense of right and wrong, empathy and compassion.

TWO

Social-Emotional Competence

Dimensions of Social-Emotional Competence

Social-emotional competence begins at birth with the attachments infants have, and the love, care and support they receive from parents and caregivers. When children develop trusting relationships with their caregivers, they begin to feel safe to express themselves, and they learn social rules and social skills through positive role models which caregivers provide (CSSP, 2018). As young children interpret their own experiences, they learn to read others' emotions and are able to develop a better understanding of how and what to do during social situations (National Scientific Council on the Developing Child, 2004). As with many lessons in life, some are easier learned than others! But, everyone--young and old alike—needs to understand that there are caring people in their lives who will help provide emotional support and a sense of belonging in what might otherwise feel like a challenging society.

The Center for the Study of Social Policy (2018) offers the following "dimensions of social-emotional competence in early childhood":

- *self-esteem: good feelings about oneself*

- *self-confidence: being open to new challenges and willing to explore new environments*

- *self-efficacy: believing that one is capable of performing an action*

- *self-regulation/self-control: following rules, controlling impulses, acting appropriately based on the context*

- *personal agency: planning and carrying out purposeful actions*

- *executive functioning: staying focused on a task and avoiding distractions*

- *patience: learning to wait*

- *persistence: willingness to try again when first attempts are not successful*

- *conflict resolution: resolving disagreements in a peaceful way*

- *communication skills: understanding and expressing a range of positive and negative emotions*

- *empathy: understanding and responding to the emotions and rights of others*

- *social skills: making friends and getting along with others*

- *morality: learning a sense of right and wrong*

Children are dependent on people in their environment to help them develop each of these skills.

There are a number of important techniques that help children develop self-esteem and self-confidence. Here, we cover separation anxiety, learning to say 'goodbye', ways to validate children's feelings, working with their needs for encouragement, their fear of failing and making mistakes, and ways to help children learn and develop self-control and self-regulation.

Self-Esteem and Self-confidence

Our three year old son has a difficult time saying goodbye to me when I drop him off at the childcare center. As a result, I end up crying and have to hide and rush out when he is not looking so that he will settle down. His teacher tells me that he stops crying when I leave. He likes his teachers, and he likes school. He is always very excited to tell me all about what he has done when I pick him up at the end of the day. Is this normal?

Separation Anxiety

Yes, this is normal. Children exhibit "separation anxiety" as early as eight months (Ceder, 2019). This is a healthy reaction because during your child's first years of life, he is just beginning to distinguish between strangers and adults. Keep in mind that when you are upset and he sees you crying, your son may think it is time to be upset, thereby adding to his distress. In any case, many children have a difficult time separating from their parents when they first begin school. Once your son makes connections, develops a trusting relationship with his teachers, makes friends and becomes more comfortable with routines, you will likely see a decrease in his distress. In the meantime, prior to leaving for childcare you might remind him about all of the things he is enjoying at school and remind him that his friends and teacher are waiting for him.

Always Say Goodbye

Your son now understands his parents are separate individuals from him and that you will leave, but he may not necessarily understand that you will return (Ceder, 2019). It is therefore very important that you ALWAYS say goodbye and tell him that you will be back soon. Give him a concrete timeline for your return so that he understands. For instance, say to him, "I will be back when you wake up from your nap" or "after you have lunch…"

In the classroom we often use funny phrases to say goodbye

at the end of our day. We have provided a list in Appendix B. For example, "See you later, alligator." You might pick a phrase from the list each day to decide how you and he can say goodbye to each other. You might also share the list with your son's caregiver so that he or she can choose a goodbye phrase when your son leaves childcare at the end of the day.

My daughter is very shy and does not like to try new things. I worry about her because she does not seem to have any confidence in herself. Do you have any suggestions for ways I might help her develop some self-confidence.

Validate Your Child's Feelings

Psychologists (Carducci, 2008) suggest that shyness is tied to an infant's temperament at birth, which often makes him or her prone to excessive reactions to environmental stimulation. Excessive reactions can lead to more anxiety and fear than the average child might experience. Your daughter needs your support and comfort to reassure her that everything is okay. Simply telling her that "Everything is okay; there is nothing to be afraid of" does not make it so. Fear and anxiety are real, no matter what age. So, instead of saying, "Everything is okay", try talking with her about her resistance to trying new things. This could help you both better understand the currently unknown cause of her anxiety or fear. It is important that you validate her feelings. For example, you can say and ask, "I can see that you are feeling upset, scared. Can you tell me what I can do to help you feel better?"

Praise Versus Encouragement

We all know that nothing builds confidence like accomplishing something worthwhile and that praise and encouragement go a long way towards building self-confidence and self-esteem. Unfortunately, we are often guilty of complimenting children on *everything* they do with "Good job!"

Think about it: If every time your daughter gets up in time for school you praise her by saying, "Good job", after several mornings it will become an expected, routine response from you. Then, when she learns that she has made the soccer team and you also say to her "Good job", it may not feel sufficient for such an important event. Instead of praising her with "Good job" on both occasions, encourage her by giving her explicit replies to her accomplishments with statements like, "Oh my goodness, you've woken every day this week for school; that's a record!" Or, "Wow, you were so worried about trying out and you made the team! You must be so proud; I'm proud of you for working so hard!"

It is always best to give particular attention to the task at hand, rather than simply praising a job well done. When used often, praise may become an expectation; when it is not regularly received it can become a disappointment. Encouragement, on the other hand, keeps specific behaviors on track independent of continued praise.

Everyone Makes Mistakes

Finally, consider that in their young years, children are afraid of failure because they want to please everyone, and with so much to learn, they will make mistakes (Gartrell, 1995). Because young children have little experience observing adults making mistakes, they might think that we never fail. Let your daughter know that everyone makes mistakes and that we can all learn from our mistakes. Share stories with your daughter about times that you've made mistakes and missed challenges. Make it a point to do something wrong purposefully on occasion so she can see it first-hand. And, model solutions to your mistake by apologizing or by otherwise taking responsibility for any negative behavior. You'll be amazed when words you've spoken to your daughter come back to you, "It's okay, we all make mistakes!"

Feelings and Emotions

Everyone experiences a range of emotions and feelings. As adults we have had years of experience learning how to both recognize and manage our emotions. Young children have had little experience and often do not really know why they are upset. It is important that they understand that we all have feelings. Responding in a positive way to those feelings determines our emotional competence. We must help them learn what they are experiencing by giving them words for it. If someone tells your son that he doesn't want to play his game, he might cry because he doesn't understand and wonders why his friend doesn't like him. You might say to him, "Your feelings are hurt because you really wanted to play, but your friend doesn't want to play that game right now. Maybe he wants to play with you, but he wants to play something else. Maybe you and he can talk about what you both want to play together. What do you think?" These dialogs go a long way toward helping young

children put words to what they are feeling and provide context for their experiences.

Sometimes it is helpful to pair a picture or photo with the corresponding "feeling" word. "I can see that you are very upset, your face is like this..." As children understand emotions better, they become more capable of regulating their emotions. And to help them learn that we all have feelings, and that we do understand, it is important to validate emotions in the moment.

Self-Control and Self-Regulation

Some believe that educating children means teaching them how to read, how to calculate mathematics, and how to strengthen other academic tasks on a competitive level. It is the opinion of the authors that when focusing our young children's education on competitive academic status, we lose crucial opportunities to focus on areas of early childhood development, including—and perhaps especially—social-emotional wellness. Too much focus on academics is counter-productive; we have to be emotionally ready to learn. As special educators we know your children will eventually learn all necessary academics, but it is imperative that we help them learn ways to appropriately navigate their social world beginning at a very young age.

Many of our students carry "baggage" into the classroom. Baggage is a term we use widely to remind us that we do not always know what happened before a student enters a classroom. We have seen students at risk for many reasons; those who have daily challenges and those who have simply had a rough morning. The range of issues and challenges are as broad as the differences in temperament we discussed earlier. Before we can expect a child to learn, we must provide him or her with understanding, a sense of belonging and emotional support.

As parents, we understand this is particularly challenging. As special educators, this is an area of development on which we focus daily. Any child who exhibits negative behaviors at home or elsewhere deserves guidance in understanding right from wrong, ways to properly exhibit socially-acceptable behaviors, and strategies for self-regulating emotions. This is important for a child's own safety and for those around him or her.

Mistakes Versus Misbehavior

As they are beginning to learn about their social world, children make mistakes. Often, however, these mistakes are misinterpreted as misbehavior (Gartrell, 1995). As discussed earlier, children do not often have the words to express what they are feeling, nor do they know how to use socially appropriate responses to problems. As a result, they might hit, kick, or take something they want from another child. As adults we know these responses are inappropriate, and we misconstrue them as "misbehavior." Young children do not necessarily know what is inappropriate behavior. As such, they make "mistakes." It is up to families and caregivers to *guide children's behavior* by helping them understand when they make mistakes, and to help them learn what they might have done to solve their problems in different ways. Early childhood specialists (Gartrell,

1995) suggest that discipline criticizes children for unacceptable behavior, while guidance helps them learn positive alternatives—or new appropriate behaviors.

Our family schedules are often chaotic as my husband and I live separately and our daughter spends weeks at a time with each of us. She has a difficult time making the weekly transitions and changes in schedules, and we are at a loss. How might we help her make these changes?

Follow Routines

Many families share your concern. Young children need routines. They need to know what to expect as much in advance as possible so that they can make some sense of their young lives (Roberts, 2014). While your schedules are varied, there are routines which can and should be consistent. These include waking and bedtime schedules, meal schedules, transport to childcare, activities, and school schedules.

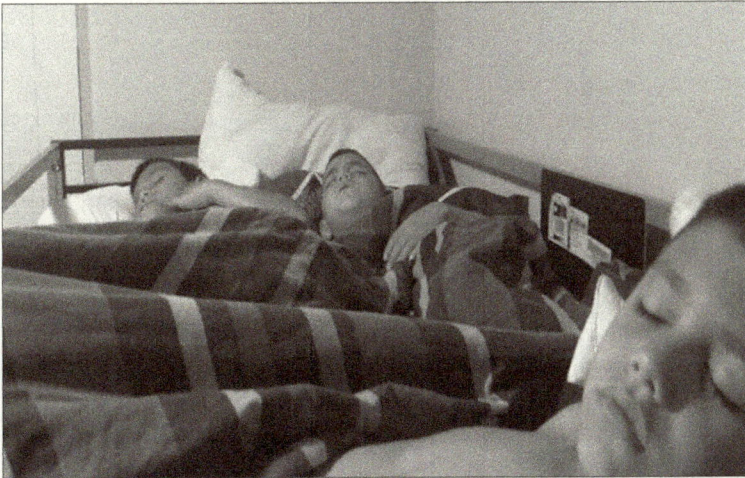

Bedtime schedules and routines are extremely important for children. Consider the same bath time and bedtime routines at both homes, including bath time followed by a bedtime routine of reading to your child and then lights out. Neurologists (Marcus, 2020) report that, among many other health benefits, the brain needs time to be able to process what it has learned during the day, and sleep is the time when it's better able to do that processing. Physicians (WebMD, 2011) recommend the following: one to three year old children should be receiving 12-14 hours of sleep in 24 hours, including one or two naps per day; three to six year old children should be receiving 10-12 hours of sleep in 24 hours, including one nap per day; and seven to twelve year old children should be receiving 10-11 hours of sleep in 24 hours.

Down Time

In addition to a good night of sleep, children need "down time." After following your rules, your schedules, and your routines, your daughter has little time to do what she chooses to do. Make sure she is getting some "down time." Allow her some quiet time in a favorite place to sit and play without interruption.

Disrupted Routines

When a routine is disrupted, adjustments or temporary changes are required. Let your child know well in advance of the changes so that she has ample time to process the new information and prepare herself emotionally for the change. Young children often become anxious when things are not as they expect them to be, and they need the regular structure of the day to help self-regulate emotions and behaviors. You might consider helping your daughter make a calendar of upcoming events. You might also take pictures of her engaged in her routines and special events, pictures of you and your spouse, school, meals, bedtime, etc. Then each evening talk about plans for the next day while she puts the pictures in order in advance of the next day's schedule. This not only allows her to better understand the daily schedule, but it also provides her some sense of control over her schedule.

Scheduling is an issue for our family as well. Every morning my daughter argues with me over breakfast, argues over what to wear, etc. As a result, I am often late for work, and she is late for school.

Give Children Choices

I doubt there is any family who hasn't experienced these moments. As adults, we often forget what it is like for a young child to continue to have to follow our leads. They have to follow our routines, our rules, and our schedules. They have little opportunity to make their own choices. While we do not always have full choices in life, we can compromise. You know your child has to get dressed and has to have breakfast, so that is not a choice. However, you might provide your daughter with choices that she can make. You might have two things available for breakfast, and ask her which she prefers: "Do you want this cereal, or yogurt?" If there are no choices, you can always ask in what color bowl she wants her cereal—anything to give her some control over her breakfast.

Getting dressed works in the same way. Instead of deciding for her, or letting her look through her entire closet, you might get two or three different outfits out and ask her which one she wants to wear. It might be easier for both of you if you help her make the decision the night before, so the clothes that she's chosen are in place in the morning. If your daughter needs to wear a jacket or sweater but won't put it on, instead of forcing her, ask her which arm she wants to put in the coat first and make a game of it. Try to find as many opportunities during the day for your daughter to make her own choices, no matter how simplistic.

I feel as though I am always yelling at my son to get him to do things and he doesn't listen!

Speak in the Positive

We like to call that "selective hearing" and it is not at all uncommon! It is difficult to maintain a steady voice and self-composure when things are "out of control." If we raise our voices, our children raise their voices. It takes practice to maintain a calm voice and self-composure. Keep in mind that children mimic our voices and our behaviors.

So, let's talk about *effective communication* with young children as they continue to develop language skills. When you want to communicate behavior expectations, those expectations must be clearly understood. Instead of telling your son what you DO NOT want him to do, tell him what you DO want him to do. Here are some examples (Lentini, Vaughn & Vox, 2005): Instead of telling him "Don't run" tell him to "Walk"; instead of telling him he will not go outside until his jacket is on, tell him "When you get your jacket on we will go outside"; instead of "Don't touch", say "Look with your eyes"; and instead of "Stop yelling", say "Use your quiet voice." It takes practice to learn to give positive instructions and to model those instructions with your own "quiet voice"!

Be Consistent

We often get so busy that it is easier to do things for our children instead of waiting for them to do them on their own—even when they are using "selective hearing." It is also often easier to give in to what a child wants rather than listen to the screams and tantrums. This does NOT work. By doing things that our children are capable of doing themselves, we are encouraging dependency. And, by giving in to temper tantrums we are setting ourselves up for even more tantrums and noncompliant behaviors as children get older and stronger. Children are smart enough to know that if a tantrum works once, it will again... and again... Be consistent. Stick with your messages: "Mean what you say," and remember that "No" means no!

THREE

Social Skills and Interaction

Development of Social Skills

As in all areas of development, social skills follow a sequence. The sequence begins when infants develop a strong attachment with significant caregivers. The young toddler begins to engage in "joint attention" by using gestures and gazes to share his attention to interesting events and objects. When a caregiver is not present, the young toddler may engage in "separation protest." When unfamiliar people try to engage with a toddler or preschool child, he or she may exhibit "stranger anxiety."

Theory of Mind

As they grow, young children also develop a "theory of mind" which is the ability to understand another person's perspective, what someone else is thinking, and to interpret what they are saying. Through theory of mind, young children begin to make sense of others' behaviors, which helps them predict what might happen next (Allen & Cowdery, 2015).

What do you mean exactly by social skills?

Social Skills

Psychologists (Kennedy-Moore, 2020) agree that there are many different definitions of social skills and that a range of skills is necessary to get along with others and to understand how to establish and maintain relationships with other people. As we reviewed in Chapter One, social skills begin in early childhood when infants smile, laugh, and respond positively to touch or to when their names are called. They are interactively becoming aware of a social world outside of themselves.

Gordon and Williams (2010) outline the "Four Hows" of social skills children learn in early years:

- How to approach: Get in and be included;

- How to interact: Sharing and cooperating;

- How to deal with difference: Teasing, bullying, including and helping others; and

- How to manage conflict: Problem solving and handling aggression.

How Children Learn Social Skills

Children develop social skills through shared experiences and by observing people in their environment, beginning in their home environment and cultural context. It is important that adults model appropriate behavior and verbal communication to children. **Families and caregivers must understand that children hear language and repeat it; they see behavior modeled and they follow it.** They are very literal learners. Take a minute to read the passage *Children Learn What They Live* by Dorothy Law Nolte on page 13, which is a brief synopsis on how a child's environment influences his social-emotional understanding.

As special educators we work with families to help their children develop social skills inside and outside of the classroom. These skills include the following:

- How to be part of a group;

- How to make friends;

- How to understand and follow rules and routines;

- How to appropriately resolve conflicts;

- How to wait patiently;

- How to take turns;

- Ways of showing empathy toward others;

- How to accept limits; and

- Ways to self-regulate their own behaviors.

In our community of learners, we work diligently to help each child feel "emotionally safe."

What do you mean by emotionally safe?

Young children are just beginning to learn about themselves and others. It is important that they know they have friends and that there are people who like them and care about them. They feel "emotionally safe" when they feel a strong sense of "belonging" and are able to freely express themselves. To feel emotionally safe, children must understand that while people may share certain similarities, they are nevertheless different. We can teach them that while some people may look and think about things the same way, others may look and think about things differently. Together, however, all people have much to learn about their similarities and differences as one people.

How can I help my son learn to develop friendships?

Developing Friendships

Interactions with others are sometimes difficult for very young children. When you add to interactions with others the need to recognize and respond to their needs and emotions with polite vocabulary and to an open sharing of their interests, making friends can be quite challenging (VDOE, 2007).

As indicated earlier, social skills are learned; children need constant coaching from adults on finding creative ways to make new friends. You can help your son by giving him empathetic language to use when talking to a new friend. In the classroom, when we see children developing friendships, we like to follow up on that lead by informing their families about those budding friendships. That way, their families can share contact information with each other and set up a "play date."

Children are comfortable in their own living space. Inviting someone to play with them sets them up for a very personal relationship in which they can share their toys and home experiences. Having your son's peer in your home also provides you with opportunities to oversee his play and perhaps coach it if the need arises. Consider asking your son's teacher if there is someone with whom he enjoys playing and who might be a good candidate for a play date.

My son is an only child. When friends come to visit he has a fit when they want to play with his toys. How do I encourage him to share?

Sharing

Sharing is a very important social skill. When we share something we are participating in the give and take of social interaction. When children are very young, toys and activities mean much more to them than how someone else feels. While aggression instead of sharing might work for children in the short term, they *must* learn, however, how to settle conflicts without aggression (VDOE, 2007). Educators (Kjesbo, 2010) recommend that adults encourage sharing by:

- Being a role model and explaining that you want to share something with someone to make them happy;

- Showing them ways to share, by playing with them and sharing things you enjoy;

- Using timers, singing a song, or counting while they wait for someone to take a turn for a short period of time;

- Using toys that encourage sharing (board games, etc.);

- Practicing reciprocal games such as rolling a ball back and forth while emphasizing, "My turn, your turn"; and

- Acknowledging when your child shares.

Sharing must be learned, and it takes a lot of patience and coaching to help children learn such an important skill.

Put Special Toys in a Special Place

If your child has particular special items that he consistently does not want to share when friends visit, you might suggest that he put them away, out of sight, before his friends arrive. However, he should understand he may not get them out while his friends visit unless he is willing to share them.

How do I help my son understand that many of the choices I make are for his own good. Although he is only five, he is constantly screaming, "That's not fair!"

Following Rules

This is a case where validating your child's feelings may help him sort out his anger. Help him to express his feelings. "You think I am not being fair; Why?" Let him know that you understand how he feels. Explain that there are times when you cannot do what you want to do and you often feel that is unfair. Remind him of times when he does get to do what he wants.

It sounds as though you might also benefit from having a set of family rules. We all have written and unwritten rules to guide us through life. As adults, we've come to understand rules from years of positive and negative experiences. Young children, on the other hand, have had little experience learning the reasons for rules. As such, rules for very young children should be few, general, easy to understand and stated in positive language: "eyes are for watching, ears for listening."

In the classroom we have rules that we often share with families for them to use at home as well. Some of the rules that we've used include the following: *be safe, be kind, and follow directions.* The goal is to have a set of umbrella rules which will cover most incidents. Some examples include:

- Your child is hitting a glass window trying to get someone's attention, you might say, "Stop. The glass might break and that would not be safe. Remember our rule? Be safe; I don't want you to be hurt."

- You hear a child say, "You can't come to my birthday party" you might say, "Be kind. Telling someone they cannot be at your party will hurt his/her feelings. We are all friends here. Remember our rule, "Be kind."

- The baby is sleeping and you've asked your son to play quietly. He then begins running around screaming. You might ask, "Are you following the directions? Remember, use your quiet voice, the baby is sleeping. Remember our rule, follow the directions."

Ask for More Time in Responding to Some Requests

There are undoubtedly times when your son asks for your permission to do something, or to have something, and you are not immediately sure how to reply. An example: you often take your son and friends to the park across the street. One day when you are busy with something else, he wants to go with his friends by himself. You know he's never gone without you, so you are a bit concerned. In this instance, you might say to him, "Let me think about it a little bit before I make a decision. I have always gone with you, so, I'm trying to think about how this might work." This way, you know he understands your concern. After you think it through and you know he will be safe with all of the other families, you tell him that he may go, as long as he stays with the group. Stress the family rule by telling him, "I want you to be safe. Remember our family rule—be safe." Don't ever feel that you need to answer right away; it's always better to have made the right decision.

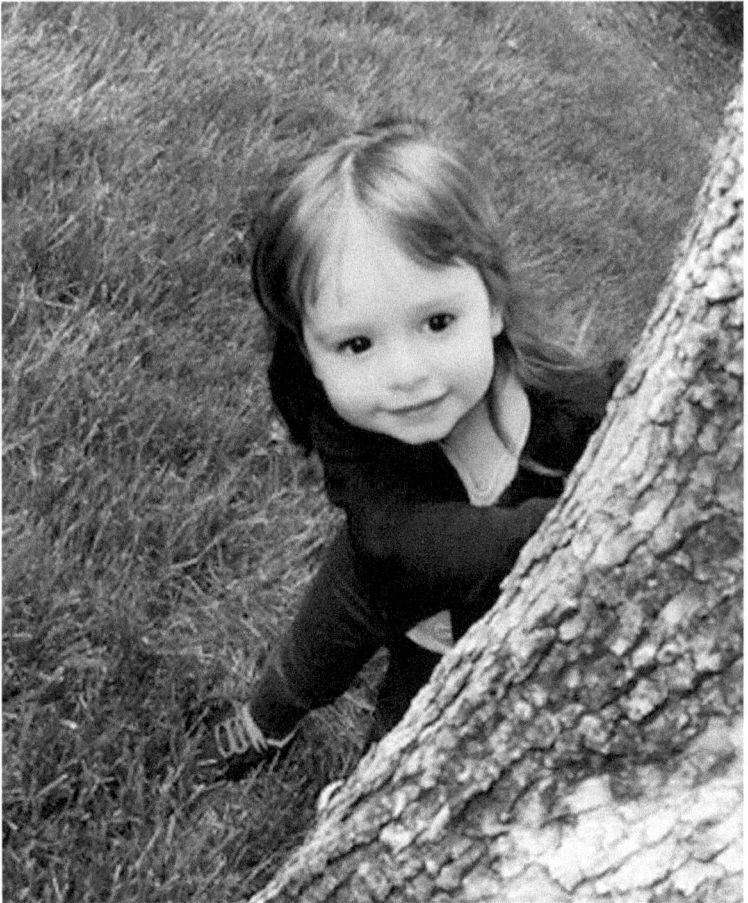

FOUR

Red Flags in Social-Emotional Development

How would I know if my child's social-emotional development is or is not developing appropriately?

Red Flags in Social-Emotional Development

There are many "red flags" when it comes to a child's social-emotional development. Psychologist Rebecca Kieffer (2002) outlines the most common areas of concern as follows:

Separation Anxiety

- Extreme distress (crying, tantrums, clinging to you) when separating from you or knowing that they will be away from you.

- The symptoms last for several months versus several days.

- The symptoms are excessive enough that it is impacting normal activities (school, friendships, and family relationships).

- The continuation or recurrence of intense anxiety upon separation after the age of 4 and through the elementary school years.

Social Concerns

- Little interest in playing with other children.

- Poor body awareness that impacts relationships with peers.

- Failure to initiate or to participate in activities.

- Difficulty making eye contact with others.

Behavioral Problems

- *Defiance:*

   Failure to follow rules or listen to directions and is often argumentative with adults.

- *Overly Aggressive Behavior*:

  Temper tantrums that last more than 5 to 10 minutes; and

  Excessive anger through threats, hitting, biting, and scratching others, pulling hair, slamming/throwing objects, damaging property, and hurting others.

Difficulty with Transitions Between Activities

- Difficulty focusing and listening during transitions.

- Extremely upset when having to transition from one activity to another. Before or during each transition, your child may cry excessively or have temper tantrums that last more than 5 to 10 minutes.

Excessive Clingingness or Attention-Seeking with Adults

- Excessive anxiety related to being around new and/or familiar people/situations.

- Child freezes or moves towards you by approaching you backwards, sideways, or hiding behind you. Your child behaves this way in most situations and no matter how you support them, they continue to avoid interacting with others.

Attention Concerns

- Difficulty completing tasks and following directives on a daily basis.

- Easily distracted and has difficulty concentrating or focusing on activities.

Daily Functioning Concerns

- *Toileting:* Difficulty potty training and refuses to use the toilet.

- *Eating issues*: Refuses to eat, avoids different textures, or has power struggles over food.

- *Sleeping problems:* Difficulty falling asleep, refuses to go to sleep, has nightmares or wakes several times at night.

School Concerns

We have had many families remind us that they often do not see these "red flags" before they hear about their child's challenges in school. As special educators, we not only understand our responsibility to our families, but we also feel a responsibility to advocate for each of the children in our charge. Before we communicate with the family about their child's red flag behaviors, we spend time observing these behaviors for a short period of time trying to understand their cause(s). It is important that families and educators communicate regularly. When you receive communications from school about the onset of a behavior of concern, take them seriously and request a meeting with the teacher. On the other hand, if you are seeing behaviors which concern you at home that may not yet be evident to your child's teacher, share them with your child's teacher. This communication is important, because if early intervention is required everyone can share in the process before the behaviors in question begin to escalate.

Challenging Behavior

As children "test" their social-emotional boundaries, challenging behaviors are considered a normal course of development. Research (Kaiser & Rasminsky, 1999) confirms that by the age of three, most children will have learned how to appropriately meet their social-emotional needs. Beyond that age, they suggest that some behaviors are considered challenging if they:

- Interfere with a child's development and success at play;

- Are harmful to the child, other children, or adults; and

- Place a child at high risk for later social problems or school failure.

My son is five and is still having regular temper tantrums. He has been dismissed from two day care centers this year because he kicks and hits when he is angry. How can I learn what brings on the tantrums?

Preparation and Collaboration with Medical and School Professionals

We would first recommend that you work with the school and your son's medical teams to try to learn what might trigger your son's behaviors, and how those behaviors might be addressed. Challenging behaviors are exhibited when we want something, are trying to avoid something, or our sensory issues are proving bothersome (Roberts, 2014). Often children do not know or cannot readily understand the source of their anger, so we are challenged with trying to "investigate" the source(s). Do a little bit of your own investigating at home to see if you recognize any patterns of difficulty in your child's behavior.

To prepare for a meeting with professionals, try asking yourself these questions: What happened? When did it happen? How often does it happen? Try following the steps ABC wherein: A stands for "antecedent"—what happened before the temper tantrum?; B is for "behavior"—what behavior is exhibited?; and C stands for "consequence"—what was done to help rectify the situation, or what was the natural consequence? These ABCs might be as simple as:

A. What happened?

B. Your child kicked another child

C. You intervene to de-escalate the situation

Very often we do not immediately know or may misconstrue what precipitated a particular action (A). This is where we need to do some investigation. In the scenario above, let's assume neither child knows why the other is reacting. We only know that your child kicked another (B). You ask him why and he says, "I want that ball." So, you ask the other child what happened and he replies, "He kicked me." This is when you should try to help them each find the words to help solve their problem (C). You might say, "You both wanted the ball? Tell my son that you don't like it when he kicks you, and he can have the ball when you are finished." Then say to your son, "So, you kicked him because you wanted to play with the ball?" To help him resolve his problem, provide him with words such as, "Ask your friend if you may play with the ball when he is finished playing with it." While this may seem simplistic, we don't always know what the child learns from kicking or being kicked, and often explicit or suppressed anger can be diffused if we take some time to listen and understand. Like any lesson, it takes practice and persistence to get the message across. Again, if your son's behavior continues to place at risk his play, development, and learning, you should seek professional assistance to better understand his behaviors.

Attention-Seeking Behavior

While it can be quite challenging, try not to take your son's behavior personally. It's difficult for adults, but we need to let go of the feeling that our children's behaviors are directed at us. Instead, view the behaviors as a way of communicating a need. What is my son seeking? Later, when he is calm, you might discuss the incident with your son to help him learn a more socially appropriate alternative to the misguided behavior.

My son doesn't seem to be able to read my feelings, nor does he seem to care about the feelings of others and often blurts out inappropriate comments about people and things. I don't understand this hurtful behavior.

I'm sure this is difficult for you. Let's begin by reviewing some of the earlier information presented on early social-emotional development. You may recall reading in the social-emotional milestones (Morin, 2020) that by six months of age, children begin to respond to others' emotions by crying, smiling, or laughing. And by seven to eight years old they become more aware of others' perceptions. As young children begin to interpret their own experiences, they learn to read the emotions of others and are able to develop a better understanding of how and what to do during social situations (National Scientific Council on the Developing Child, 2004). Through the theory of mind, when young children begin to make sense of the behaviors of others, they are better able to predict what might happen next (Allen & Cowdery, 2015). If these theories are part of early childhood social-emotional development, and your son does not exhibit understanding in these areas, it may very well be indicative of a red flag in his development. We would suggest that you contact a developmental physician to address your concerns.

Meanwhile, continue to validate his feelings while focusing on areas of concern to help him develop some aspect of the theory of mind. It is likely that he does not understand that his mind works differently than others (Roberts, 2014). He might assume that everyone has the same thoughts and thinks the same way at the same time that he is having his particular thoughts. Remind him when he is acting or speaking inappropriately that you understand how he is feeling, but that not everyone feels the same way that he does. If he is having a difficult time reading your feelings, it may help if you tell him as well as show him how you are feeling. For instance, say to him, "I am angry, see my face? This is an angry face." Or, "I am so happy, see my smile. My smile is a happy face" (Roberts, 2014).

My son wants his tablet all of the time and has temper tantrums when we do not let him play on it. Is that typical?

Screen Time

Screen time has been debated for many years. Indeed, television time was scrutinized because children were spending a couple of hours a day watching television. But, while television screens paved the way for watching videos on car trips and on laptop computers, they were not as portable, Internet accessible, or as widely received as the current screens we now have available to us in tablets and smartphones. If you consider that through his environment in real time your son is developing social-emotional skills as well as learning how to make social connections while engaging in social communication, you might better understand why screen time may be negatively affecting his social-emotional development and contributing to his temper tantrums. When he is using his tablet, he is removed from his social environment. Your child is not communicating or interacting with another person. For this reason, screen time should be carefully monitored and restricted.

Psychologists (Dunkley, 2019) report that by literally changing brain function, screen time promotes inappropriate behaviors. To minimize the negative effects of screen time, pyschologist Dunkley suggests full removal from electronics and then a gradual return to limited screen time. Among the negative effects cited in the report were:

- disruption of sleep and disruption of the "body clock" because blue light from the device mimics daylight. Our bodies need the chemical melatonin to sleep and just a few minutes of screen time delays the release of melatonin. The brain becomes inflamed and all kinds of unhealthy bodily functions occur, including arousal, which do not permit the body to engage in a deep sleep;

- screen time gaming increases the chemical dopamine, which our bodies produce when we feel good. In fact, the amount of dopamine released during a good game session is shown on a brain scan to be equivalent to that of a person using cocaine. When that feel-good brain pathway is used to such an excess, the body becomes less sensitive to it, so that it requires more and more stimulation to feel good. Although there are undoubtedly fewer things in his real world that will give a child the same amount of instant gratification as tablet gaming, there are well documented negative effects of too much tablet gaming;

- causes depression: there is a "night at light" theory which indicates that exposure from the screen light before or during sleep causes depression;

- increases stress reactions which can increase irritability;

- overloads the sensory system causing a person to lack attention, while depleting mental reserves; and

- reduces the need for physical activity and takes away the many opportunities children have to interact with nature and reduce aggression.

Considering these negative findings, you might want to monitor the amount of time your son uses his tablet, reduce the time he uses it, and watch for any changes in his behavior at home. Try setting a timer for using the tablet and, when it sounds, switch to another activity. It will no doubt be difficult to restrict use at first, but perhaps using the tablet as a reward will work. Use FIRST/THEN language, for instance: "FIRST, we will go to the store, and THEN, when we get home you can use the tablet for fifteen minutes."

A note of caution: Physicians (MedLine, 2020) agree that children under the age of two should *not* engage in screen time and that children over two years old should be limited to one to two hours a day for screen time. They further report that despite what you might hear, videos that are aimed at very young children do NOT improve their development.

I don't know what causes it, but my daughter is very non-compliant both at school and at home. The school is suggesting an FBA and a possible BIP. Can you tell me what that means?

A functional behavior analysis (FBA) is a collection of data over a period of time to learn what happens before, during, and after a behavior incident, along with the time of day, the number of occurrences in a period of time, and the length of time a behavior persists. The purpose of the FBA is to track the behavior to learn what your child is seeking through his behavior, and to learn as much as possible so that everyone involved can determine if there is a need to put a Behavior Intervention Plan (BIP) in place. If you and others on the education team determine that a BIP would be helpful to your child, together you would draft a behavior plan to be put in place at home and in the classroom. The plan would include strategies to address a specific behavior in order to decrease incidents and/or to eliminate a specific behavior of concern. When putting a BIP in place, the goal is to find a replacement behavior that will meet the same needs of the interfering behavior.

My son regularly has what we describe as "meltdowns." He screams and cries for long periods of time and we are not able to calm him. What suggestions might you offer to help him calm?

These meltdowns that you describe are worrisome. I hope you are getting advice from medical and behavior specialists. Understand that we are special educators and not behavior specialists or psychologists, so advice on extreme anger and calming strategies would be better addressed by those specialists.

Any suggestions we can provide are from our own classroom experiences. First of all, you must validate your understanding of your son's emotion—that he is upset, that you see him crying. In the classroom, we often practice breathing techniques to help children calm. We teach the children as a group, and then when a child is in emotional crisis, we calmly remind him to follow our lead: deep breath in, hold it. . .blow it out. In our experience younger children respond better to pictures of breathing techniques (Willey, 2017). For instance, a picture of a field of flowers with the prompt to "Smell all of the flowers" means take a deep breath in. A picture of a birthday cake with several candles and the prompt, "Now blow out all of the candles", suggests let out a deep breath.

It may be that your son has no idea why he gets so upset. When he is comfortable and not upset, take some quiet time together to discuss feelings and strategies he used in the past to help himself feel better. Read to him books about different feelings so that he understands he is not the only one who gets upset. You can find many children's books on emotions in the public library or on the Internet. Some of our favorites include:

When Sophie Gets Angry (Bang, M., Scholastic Inc.)

Glad Monster/Sad Monster (Emberly E., & Miranda A., Scholastic Books)

Llama, Llama, Mad at Mama (Dewdney, A. Viking Books)

Mean Soup (Everitt, B., Voyager Books)

On Monday When it Rained (Kachenmeister, C. & Berthiaume, T. Houghton Mifflin Co.)

Sometimes I'm Bombaloo (Vail, R. Heyo., Y., Scholastic Press)

The Feelings Book (Parr, T., Little Brown & Company)

What if I have concerns about my child's social-emotional development?

As with any delay in development, you should first make an appointment with your child's developmental physician. If your physician shares your concern, contact your local government

jurisdiction for family services. Every jurisdiction has a child services office for preschool children. Some common names for the programs are: the Infant Toddler Connection (ITC), the Parent and Infant Education (PIE) program and/or preschool Child Find. Through these programs, your child can be evaluated for potential developmental delays. Once your child begins kindergarten, however, screening can be requested by you through your child's public school.

Our Advice to Parents about Early Social-Emotional Development

Educators often have plenty of advice to offer parents about things they should be doing at home with their children to help them with their social-emotional development. At times, parents must feel frustrated by the advice. Often, families with whom we work hope that their children will adopt better social-emotional competencies simply by being in a classroom social environment.

Being in any social environment is a benefit to all children. Certainly, in an exemplary care setting, young children learn to be part of a group, to communicate socially, and to develop self-esteem as they learn along with their peers and engage in activities in a community of learners. However, as we discussed earlier in the book, temperament begins at birth. How children exhibit their emotions and social skills can be just as individual and as unique as their temperament. Social-emotional skills must be learned. Furthermore, just as we indicated in our book, *Let's Talk About Early Language Development* (Hoover & Roberts, 2013), social-emotional competencies are learned through social interactions and communications based on the rich culture, discussions, interactions and explorations which families share.

Our advice to families of young children is to provide every opportunity for rich social-emotional experiences and lessons. Take time to talk, to discuss and share ideas, and spend quality time together. Teach one another by:

- Facilitating peer interactions by modeling and by providing your child with language to support his or her interactions;

- Providing and facilitating understanding of rules and routines;

- Effectively communicating by telling your child WHAT to do instead of what NOT to do and by using "first/then" language toward positive guidance;

- Using "feelings" words to help your child understand his or her emotions and by using children's books to label feelings as you read;

- Labeling and validating your child's emotions: "You are so happy!"

- Labeling and sharing your OWN feelings, "I felt scared when...";

- Teaching replacement skills your child may use to allow him or her to escape, get attention or communicate in a way which is more socially appropriate;

- Coaching to help your child learn to solve problems in a way which is more socially appropriate;

- Modeling expected behaviors and modeling calmness. Never raise your voice at a child who is already in emotional distress;

- Using negative behaviors as an opportunity to teach appropriate behaviors (Keep in mind rewards and punishment do not teach accountability.);

- Limiting screen time with a goal to increase time for social interaction;

- Being consistent with encouragement, with understanding, with rules and routines, with modeling, and with shared behavior strategies.

Finally, understand that while some lessons are easier learned than others, life is a series of shared adventures. Enjoy the richness of life that comes with sharing a social life with your children. And let's continue to talk about early social-emotional development as educators and as parents.

Appendix A

Suggestions for Further Reading

The following publications may or may not be included in the reference section of this book, but are the authors' suggestions for further reading on topics of particular interest.

Bilmes, J. (2012). *Beyond behavior management: The six life skills children need.* (2nd Ed.) St. Paul, MN: Redleaf Press.

A wealth of information on understanding children's social-emotional development along with strategies to help them when they are struggling with self-control. This book offers many different ways for looking at behavior and better ways for us to express ourselves in order to be one step ahead of expressed mistaken behaviors in young children.

Galinsky (2010). *Mind in the making: The seven essential life skills every child needs.* New York, NY: HarperCollins.

A fantastic book for parents which outlines skills which all children need to be citizens of our often very complicated and confusing world.

Gartrell, D. (2004). *The power of guidance: Teaching social-emotional skills in early childhood classrooms.* Clifton Park, NY: Thomas Learning Inc.

As teachers and parents alike, this is a go-to book on understanding early childhood social-emotional competencies and effective strategies toward positive guidance.

Greene, R.W. (2014). *The Explosive Child: A new approach for understanding and parenting easily frustrated, chronically inflexible children.* New York, NY: HarperCollins.

For parents of children with challenging behavior issues with or without a medical diagnosis. The author's theme is "kids do well if they can." He goes through a step by step process on how to work together with your child to "solve problems" and become less frustrated.

Harvey, P. & Penzo, J. (2009). *Parenting a child who has intense emotions.* Oakland, CA: New Harbinger Publications, Inc.

This book includes "Dialectical Behavior Therapy" (DBT) skills which both provide information on reasons for behaviors, as well as provide parents strategies to help children "regulate emotional outbursts and aggressive behaviors."

Kaiser, B., Rasminsky, J. (2007). *Challenging behavior in young children: Understanding, presenting and responding effectively.* (2nd Ed.) New York, NY: Pearson, Allyn & Bacon.

Another book on ways to address mistaken behaviors in young children.

Wiley, K., & Betts, A. (2017). *Breathe like a bear: 30 Mindful moments for kids to feel calm and focused.* Emmaus, PA: Rodale Books.

A wonderful book which includes "mindfulness" exercises designed to teach kids techniques for managing their bodies, breath, and emotions. Includes simple, short breathing practices and movements.

Appendix B

Fun Ways to Say Goodbye

BLOW ME A KISS JELLYFISH

SEE YOU LATER ALLIGATOR

YOU ROCK JACK-IN-THE-BOX

NOT TOO SOON LITTLE BABOON

DON'T BE SQUARE, KOALA BEAR

ALL'S FINE PORCUPINE

BE SWEET PARAKEET

SCAT CAT

YOU AND ME BUMBLEBEE

TAKE CARE PANDA BEAR

AFTER A WHILE CROCODILE

BE BACK SOON LITTLE RACCOON

GIVE ME A HUG BUG

BYE-BYE BUTTERFLY

SCRAM CLAM

GOTTA BAIL SLIMY SNAIL

HAVE A GREAT DAY MANTA RAY

ON COURSE SEAHORSE

References

Allen, K.E., & Cowdery, G.E. (2015). *The exceptional child: inclusion in early childhood education*. Stamford, CT: Cengage Learning.

Ceder, J. (2019). *The importance of saying goodbye to your child*. Retrieved March 5, 2020 from Website: https://www.verywellfamily.come/the-importance-of-goodbyes.

Center for the Study of Social Policy (2018). *Social-emotional competence of children: Protective and promotive factors*. Retrieved July 22, 2018 from CSSP.ORG. strengtheningfamilies.net

Changing Minds (2018). *Temperament, mood and emotion*. Retrieved July 22, 2018 from Changing Minds website: http://changingminds.org/explanations/emotions/temperament_mood_emotion.htm.

Carducci, B.J. (2008). *Are we born shy? Genetics, environment, and bashfulness*. Retrieved March 20, 2020 from Psychology Today Website:https://www.psychologytoday.com/us/blog/breaking-the-ice/2000806/are-we-born-shy.

Cherry, K. (2018). *social-emotional milestones*. Retrieved June 29, 2018 from VeryWellMind website: http://www.verywellmind.com/social-and-emotional-milestones

Dunckley, V.L. (2020). *Screentime is making kids moody, crazy and lazy*. Retrieved January 29, 2020 from Psychology Today website: https://www.psychologytoday.comus/blog/mental-wealth/201508.

Gartrell, D. (2014). *A guidance approach for the encouraging classroom*. Belmont, CA: Wadsworth Cengage Learning.

Gartrell, D. (1995). *Misbehavior or mistaken behavior?* Young Children Magazine, NAEYC, Washington, DC.

Gordon, A.M., & Williams Browne, K. (2010) *Beginnings and beyond: Foundations in early childhood education*. Wadsworth, Cengage Learning: Belmont CA..

Harvey, P. & Penzo, J. (2009). *Parenting a child who has intense emotions*. Oakland, CA: New Harbinger Publications, Inc.

Hoover, A. & Roberts, K. (2013). *Let's talk about early language development*. Fourth Lloyd Productions, Burgess, VA.

Kaiser, B. & Rasminsky, J. (1999). *Meeting the challenge: Effective strategies for challenging behaviors in early childhood environments*. Ontario, Canada: Canadian Child Care Federation.

Kennedy-Moore, E. (2020). *Helping children become comfortable and competent in social situations*. Retrieved February 2, 2020 from Psychology Today Website: https://www.psychologytoday.com/us/blog/growing-friendships/201108

Kieffer, R., (2020). *Social-Emotional and Behavioral Red Flags For Toddlers and Preshcoolers*. Retrieved February 9, 2020 from Parenting Website: https://www.nspt4kids.com/specialties-and-services/mental-health/social-emotional-and-behavioral-red-flags-for-toddlers.

Kjesbo, Rynette, R. (2010). *Sharing: An important social skill*. Retrieved from Super Duper Publications Website: www.superduperinc.com.

Lentini, R, Vaughn B.J. & Fox L. (2005). *Teaching Children with Challenging Behavior*. University of South Carolina. Columbia, SC.

Marcus, D. (2020). *Why is it important for children to get enough sleep?* Retrieved February 8, 2020 from Wesley Medical Center Website: ww.sharecare.com/health/sleep-basics/important-children-enough-sleep

MedLine Plus (2020). *Screen time and children*. Retrieved from National Library of Medicine Website, March 18, 2020: https://medlineplus.gov/ency/patientinstructions/000355.htm

Morin, A. (2020). *social-emotional skills: What to expect at different ages*. Retrieved March 18, 2020 from Understood for All, Inc. Website: https://www.understood.org /en/learning-thinking-differences/signs-symptoms/age-by-age-learning-skills/social-and-emotional-skills-what-to-expect-at-different-ages

National Scientific Council on the Developing Child (2004). *Children's emotional development is built into the architecture of their brains: Working paper no. 2*. Retrieved July 22, 2018 from Harvard University website: http://www.developingchild.net.

Roberts, K.G. (2014). *Let's talk about autism in early childhood*. Fourth Lloyd Productions, Burgess, VA.

Trawick-Smith, J. (2005). *Early childhood development: A multicultural perspective*. (4th Ed.). Upper Saddle River, NJ: Prentice Hall.

Virginia Department of Education (VDOE), (2007). *Virginia's foundation blocks for early learning*. Retrieved February 14, 2020 from VDOE's website: http://www.doe.virginia.gov/VDOE/Instruction/Elem_M/FoundationBlocks.

WebMD (2011). *Child sleep: Recommend for every age*. Retrieved from Parenting website: http://www.webmd.com/parenting/guide/sleep-children.

Wiley, K., & Betts, A. (2017). *Breathe like a bear: 30 Mindful moments for kids to feel calm and focused*. Emmaus, PA: Rodale Books.

Zero to Three (2010). *Social-emotional development: 4 to 36 months*. Retrieved July 22, 2018 from Zero to Three website: www.zerotothree.org/reprint

About the Authors

M s. Roberts and Ms. Hoover authored three books in the "Let's Talk" series. The idea for the series was drawn during their years of teaching from the many questions special education families expressed about their child's challenges in early development. They co-authored the first of the series, *Let's Talk About Early Language Development* (2013). The second in the series, *Let's Talk About Autism in Early Childhood* was authored by Ms. Roberts (2014). They co-authored this final and third in the series, *Let's Talk About Early Childhood Social-Emotional Development* (2020).

Karen Griffin Roberts holds a Bachelors of Individualized Study (BIS) in Early Childhood Development: A Study in Autism, and a Masters Degree in Education with an endorsement in Early Childhood Special Education, both from George Mason University. Her undergraduate project to develop a manual for preschool teachers to use for including children with autism in the classroom won George Mason University's BIS award for "Most Creative Project," May 16, 2009 which resulted in the publication of the book, *Embracing Autism in Preschool: Successful Strategies for General Education Teachers (2010, 2020)*.

Ms. Roberts has an adult son with autism. Before teaching in public schools, she taught general education preschool for nineteen years. From 2010-2019 Ms. Roberts was employed by Prince William County Schools, first as a teacher of preschool special education students for seven years, and then for two years as a teacher of students with autism in kindergarten through second grade. She retired from full-time teaching in 2019 but continues to substitute in special education classrooms at the school's request.

Ana Gamarra Hoover holds a Bachelors of Individualized Studies (BIS) in Child Development and Early Childhood Special Education, and a Masters Degree in Education with an endorsement in Early Childhood Special Education, both from George Mason University. She is currently a full-time special educator in Prince William County Schools. Ms. Hoover is also an adjunct faculty member for Northern Virginia Community College where she has the pleasure of teaching and preparing students in the early childhood field. And, she is a consultant for McFarren Aviles and Associates LLC, a company which provides professional development, CLASS assessment and coaching for early childhood educators.

www.ingramcontent.com/pod-product-compliance
Lightning Source LLC
Chambersburg PA
CBHW030302030426
42336CB00009B/491